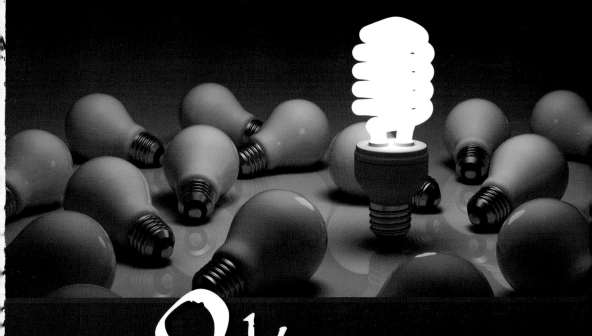

The $9\frac{1}{2}$ Principles
of Innovative Service

Book Design: Brian Frantz
Images by: ShutterStock images

Published by Simple Truths, an imprint of Sourcebooks, Inc.
P.O. Box 4410, Naperville, Illinois 60567-4410
(630) 961-3900
Fax: (630) 961-2168
www.sourcebooks.com

Printed and bound in China.
OGP 10 9 8 7 6 5 4 3

Table of Contents

The Welcome Appetizer

*F*rancie Johnsen is my very favorite pharmacist. When the petite redheaded bundle of energy first came to work at the Eckerds Pharmacy (now CVS) near my home, she encountered a store spirit painted plain vanilla. Employees were creating a completely memory-less experience. Nothing was wrong mind you—there was just nothing that would make you want to come back.

But under Francie's magical influence, the energy in the store quickly became as animated as a new puppy let out of its cage.

Francie manages customer wait in a way that leaves customers totally infatuated. "Chip," she said to me one day noticing my obvious impatience, "go check to see if your pictures are ready while I fill your script."

"But, Francie," I protested, "I don't have pictures being developed."

Unchanged by my refusal to take her bait, she elevated the fun to a higher altitude. "Well, go look at someone else's pictures–or better yet, go check your blood pressure on that machine over there. I'll have your order ready by the time you get back."

Before Francie, should you have a prescription called in or dropped off for later retrieval, you got a mechanical "someone-in-this-household-has-a-prescription-ready-for-pickup" message on your answering machine. She terminated that. When our vet called in a prescription for our cat, the answering machine at our house played an even more playful message: "Taco, meow, meow," the message trumpeted in Francie's voice, "tell your parents, meow, meow, that your prescription is ready, meow, meow!"

Not only did she call the cat, she spoke fluent kitty!

Value-added has been the service solution for many service exemplars—take what your customers expect and add a little more. But value-added extras have gotten a lot more expensive. That guest room on the hotel's fancy floor that front desk clerks used to upgrade a frequent guest, for example, now needs to be sold to generate full revenue. No more baker's dozen; the merchant needs to sell each donut with no extras. Tough economic times call for a new approach: value-unique service.

"It is the service we are not obliged to give that people value most."

-J. C. Penney

Value-unique is different from value-added. It is not about addition—"they gave me more than I anticipated." It is about a unique and unexpected creation. When service people are asked to give more, they often think, "I'm already doing the best I can." But if asked to pleasantly surprise more customers, they feel less like worker bees and more like fireflies. And when employees get to create, not just perform, they feel prized. This refreshingly novel brand of service leaves customers more than cheaply entertained— it leaves them richly stirred.

"If you work just for money, you'll never make it, but if you love what you're doing and you always put the customer first, success will be yours."

-Ray Kroc

This book is your instruction manual and inspirational guide to making service an experience that causes your customers to swoon, smile, and sing your praises. It is your sparkplug for bringing energy and igniting your customers' experiences. It is built around 9 1/2 principles to guide your practice—think of them as lenses crafted to reveal special strategies and techniques you can use to become the subject of glowing remarks! And what's a half of a principle? You'll have to wait and find out. Remember, this book is all about the unexpected!

The 9 ½ principles include:

1. **Put a Surprise Inside—The Cracker Jack Principle**

2. **Connect with Respect—The "Big Boy" Event Principle**

3. **Elevate the Class—The Purpling Principle**

4. **Put Total Sense into Service—The Speed Limit 23 MPH Principle**

5. **Before and Beyond Service—The Circus Principle**

6. **Hardwire Wisdom into Service—The Campfire Story Principle**

7. **Monogram the Moment--The Fly-Fishing Principle**

8. **Effort Removal Squared—The Easy Button Principle**

9. **Turn an Oops into an Opportunity—The Panning for Gold Principle**

½. Synergize Your Service Delivery—The Fruit Salad Principle

This book is dedicated to the quest for being remarkable. "Remarkable takes originality, passion, guts and daring," wrote Seth Godin in his best-selling book *Purple Cow*. "Not just because going through life with passion and guts beats the alternative (which it does), but because it is the only way to be successful. Today, the one sure way to fail is to be boring. Your one chance for success is to be remarkable." Get set for a unique ride ahead!

"We see our customers as invited guests to a party, and we are the hosts. It's our job every day to make every important aspect of the customer experience a little bit better."

-Jeff Bezos

And one last thing! Please don't put this book on your bookshelf after you have read it! You are not going to go back to this book as a reference. Let it benefit your colleagues or customers. Give it away! And if you want assistance or resources, my contact information is right where you'd put it—at the end of the book!

PUT A SURPRISE INSIDE

The Cracker Jack Principle

$\mathcal{W}$e bought a new house in a real nice neighborhood. The house was perfect except for one important feature—it came with a yard! I do not like yard work and my wife does not like yard work. I travel all the time and she works long hours.

One Saturday morning, I got a big idea! "Why don't we just concrete our front yard," I thought. When my wife mentioned to a friend I was considering calling the concrete trucks, word spread and a delegation of concerned neighbors showed up at our front door. It is clearly not a neighborhood with concrete front yards.

"Please, you have to hire Bill," they pleaded. "Bill does all our yards." So Bill was summoned to our house late one afternoon for an "audition."

Bill arrived in an old pickup truck loaded with garden equipment. Dressed in faded jeans, a "gimme" tee shirt from Miracle Grow® and a sweat-stained cowboy hat, he leaped out of the front seat. Grabbing a stack of pale green index cards, he ran up the sidewalk to ring the doorbell. "These caladiums are getting too much water," he announced even before introducing himself at the front door.

Invited in, Bill removed his boots and hat, leaving both on the front steps. Once inside he confidently began his inquisition and completion of his index cards. His questions were as rapid fire as his gait. "What time do you get home from work? Do you mind if your sidewalk is wet when you get home? Do you ever pick flowers from your yard to use inside? What do you folks do for fun on the weekend? When you go fishing, what do you like to catch? What's the best-looking yard in the neighborhood? Can I please have another glass of iced tea?" Bill was hired!

A month later Bill decided it was time to replace the annuals in our front yard—from summer geraniums to winter pansies. It required removing, mulching, planting and fertilizing. We came home late Thursday to find an immaculate yard. On the front door was one of Bill's signature green index cards with a note: "Go look on your back porch." Racing to the back yard, we found a large Styrofoam cup of earthworms in moist soil. On the cup Bill had penciled, "Hope you catch a big one this weekend."

Service with surprise is like a box of Cracker Jack. It was not the cool box or the caramelized popcorn we craved—it was the free prize inside. While the prize had little economic value, its emotional value was priceless. Surprise breaks the monotony of ho-hum, communicates a caring attitude, and fosters an infectious spirit that customers cannot wait to narrate to others.

Some companies have the principle of including the Cracker Jack surprise down pat.

Zappos is ranked #2 in the U.S. on customer service. It also has "Create Fun and a Little Weirdness" as one of its core values. Zappos sent a bouquet of flowers to a loyal customer after the call center operator learned she had just had an emergency appendectomy. Miller Brothers, Ltd., an upscale men's clothing store in Atlanta, has "sophisticated fun" as one of its hallmark values. And the proof? A colorful gumball machine sits on a small table in the store's entrance foyer. Beside it is a large bowl of bright shiny pennies. Guess where Junior goes while daddy is trying on trousers?

What can you do to apply the CRACKER JACK Principle? Pretend the service that you deliver is like your customer's birthday. The best gifts are those that contain a delightful surprise. Put on your "little kid" creative hat and consider ways to make your service silly, funny, whimsical or quaint. Better yet, ask a kid for ideas! Like Cracker Jack, position the surprise in a way that heightens the astonishment and amazement.

"Being on par in terms of price and quality only gets you into the game. Service wins the game."

-Tony Alessandra

"...We decided that we wanted to build our brand to be about the very best customer service and the very best customer experience. We believe that customer service shouldn't be just a department, it should be the entire company."

-Tony Hsieh, CEO, Zappos.com

"It is service that measures success."

-George Washington Carver

CONNECT WITH RESPECT

The "Big Boy" Event Principle

Two things I remember about my very first suit. It was a powder blue suit—perfect for Easter Sunday church dress-up. And it was a "big boy" event. I was seven years old. Joseph Neel's Men's Wear in Macon, Georgia, was a two-hour drive from my rural hometown and we visited only every August to buy school clothes. But this purchase required a special spring journey.

The "big boy" event started with the salesperson pulling up a chair in front of me at my eye level. He shook my hand and introduced himself by his first name, not "Mr." Without a single glance at my dad, he asked me about my favorite color. And my second favorite color. He asked me about my hobbies and wanted to know my best friend's name. We were pals in a matter of minutes. I walked out of the store very tall with a suit in my favorite color, a white dress shirt, a pair of shoes, and a tie in my second favorite color. Did I mention that I was seven?

Customers love service connections with respect. Respectful service—experiences filled with admiration—start and end with a clear and present devotion for customers. It is affirmation laced with authenticity. It is confident deference without a hint of servitude. And it is born out of enormous pride in one's role and workmanship manifested as a kind of invitation to the experience. It is as if the server is saying, "Come witness and experience my excellent work, crafted just for you." It is like a "random act of kindness," only respectful service is not random; it is perpetual.

Respectful service honors the unique situation of each customer. It shows that you not only connect with your customers—you care for them. Barry Orr, CEO of First Bank and Trust in Lubbock,

Texas, views his employees as his most important customers. He encourages employees to "not miss that special ballgame with Junior or a dental appointment." Employees are asked to simply make up the needed time off by working later or on the weekend. No one monitors it; the honor system is a powerful communication of respect.

Respectful service goes the extra mile for customers. "It was going to be a fantastic trip to Disneyworld," said my friend Bob Parsons at the Washington Speakers Bureau. "We go every year and this

"To give real service you must add something which cannot be bought or measured with money, and that is sincerity and integrity."

-Douglas Adams

year we were getting ready to make the 13-hour drive. The car was packed, the family was loaded, and we were all about ready to start singing, 'M-I-C-K-E-Y.'"

But there was no pixie dust under the hood of the Parsons family car that afternoon. The car refused to start. And it was approaching 5:00 p.m.—closing time for Safford Auto in Warrenton, Virginia, where the car is serviced.

"I called Safford Auto," Bob continued as he acted out the dialogue. "I know you folks are about to close at Safford, but here is my situation." Bob added more phone dialogue to his story. "We can get the car started with jumper cables from our other car, but the battery will need to be replaced." The Safford Auto guy told Bob, "Bring it on by. We've got a mechanic here who says he'll wait for you."

But the travel demons moved from Bob's hood to the interstate as the 5 o'clock traffic snarl made the trip to the mechanic take way longer than expected. A quick call to Safford assured Bob that the mechanic was still there and would continue to wait.

After the repair was completed and the Parsons family was ready to resume their trip to Disney, Bob asked the mechanic, who was now locking the front door, "Why did you decide to wait?" There was no vision-quoting, "We are dedicated to giving you world-

class service." There was no chest-beating, "Safford is #1 in customer satisfaction." Just a simple, straight from the heart, "You sounded like you needed help!" It was a neighbor showing respect to another neighbor!

Think of the respectful approach as "grandmother-style service." Grandmothers spoil you just because they get a kick out of it—remembering your favorite everything, always giving you a little bit extra and cheering you up when others chastise. Grandmothers believe you are still terrific even after your parents ground you. Delivering respect is the service equivalent of being your customers' grandmas.

What can you do to apply the "BIG BOY" EVENT Principle?

Use "sir" and "ma'am" to people you do not normally address in that manner. Thank someone who never gets expressions of gratitude—the janitor in the bathroom, the cashier in the checkout line, the invisible and taken-for-granted maintenance people. Listen to customers as if you were at a raffle, hoping to hear you have the winning number. Be a proactive guardian of your customers' dignity. Always do what you say you will do. Respectful service entails an extra helping of help, an enduring act of benevolence and a sincere interest in making a difference in the welfare of those around you.

"It starts with respect. If you respect the customer as a human being, and truly honor their right to be treated fairly and honestly, everything else is much easier."

-Doug Smith

"Everyone can be great…
because everyone can serve."

-Martin Luther King, Jr.

"To be successful, you have to have
your heart in your business, and your
business in your heart."

-Thomas Watson, Sr.

ELEVATE THE CLASS

The Purpling Principle

*I*t started out as a lackluster taxi ride from the airport to the hotel. But it turned regal and elegant the second I hailed the next taxi up as I exited Charlotte Douglas Airport. The Crown Cab that pulled up was shiny and spotless. When the taxi driver raised the trunk to deposit my roller bag, I was stunned to see it was lined in mink—not real mink of course, but a faux mink blanket. Instead of returning to the driver's side, he opened the passenger door for me to embark.

As the taxi pulled away, classical music began playing on the radio. There was a cup holder with a small bottle of ice cold water. The magazines in the seat were ones you might expect at a luxury hotel—*Robb Report*, *Wine Spectator* and *Town and Country*. When I complimented the driver on his choice of music and reading material, he smiled and humbly responded, "My pleasure, sir." I felt like a rich tycoon in a chauffeur-driven limousine. And it was a 10-year-old Chevrolet! I was "purpled"!

If you spend time with young granddaughters, you quickly learn the importance of the color purple. Pink is a girl color, but purple is a princess (or prince) color—a hue of nobility. The word is typically used as a noun or adjective. For granddaughters with an undying desire to be a princess, it is also a verb: "I will 'purple' you with my wand." Think of it as the six-year-old version of knighting someone. After you are "purpled," you are to be always treated as a prince or princess.

Customers love being "purpled"—raising the class and increasing the elegance of service. Servers who "purple" find ways to enrich the experience by adorning the mundane. It is the financial consultant sending papers by courier when regular mail would be adequate. It is a carwash attendant in white coveralls and a tie. Or a flight attendant placing plastic flight wings on a child's doll as well as the child as both board. It is the manicurist who walks out to open the customer's car door and start her engine so she won't scuff her nails.

Examples of the "purpling" principle are all around us—if we look for them. MedStar Health's Franklin Square Hospital Center in Baltimore commissioned a new breed of hybrid rose called the

"Rose of Hope." Each new cancer patient at the center receives a Hope rose as he or she begins treatment. Sewell Village Cadillac in Dallas decorates the service waiting room with pricey leather sofas, gourmet coffee and pastries; its elegant bathrooms have fresh flowers. Catalyst Ranch, a meeting center in Chicago, keeps three brands of LCD projectors to ensure compatibility with any laptop.

Legend has it that in the mid-1600s when Dom Perignon invented what we know today as champagne, he called to his friends and exclaimed (in French, of course), "Come quickly, I am tasting the stars!" "Purpling" is a deliberate rebellion against plain vanilla service. It is helping your customers "taste the stars."

"Always give the customer more
than they expect."

-Nelson Boswell

What can you do to apply the PURPLING principle? Create service processes that ensure red-carpet ease, not a thorn-filled path of excess effort, unexpected dissonance, and policies written in the language of distrust. Care about customers as special people not simply as subjects who are but a means to revenue. Remove those spirit leeches who try to suck the ecstasy and elegance out of work by showing them your red-hot passion.

"It's the little things that make the big things possible. Only close attention to the fine details of any operation makes the operation first class."

-J. Willard Marriott

Boldly summon customers on a journey to collective joy much like a child welcoming a close friend to a tree house filled with secrets.

Put Total Sense into Service

The Speed Limit 23 MPH Principle

*I*magine a hotel proposing that the housekeeper put a goldfish in your guest room in a basketball-sized bowl filled with colorful rocks. All they ask is that you give it a name so you can have "your" fish join you again on your next stay. Visualize the bathrobe in the closet being zebra or leopard-colored and not boring white or the turn-down item left on your pillow something completely unexpected—a foreign coin, a flower, even a lottery ticket—instead of the proverbial mint. Welcome to the Hotel Monaco!

Hotel Monaco is my favorite hotel. Not only because of its over-the-top service but because it provides a clever cacophony of sensory stimulations. Your colorful guest room radiantly greets you with garden-fresh flowers, peaceful fragrances, unusual artwork and restful music. Bathroom amenities range from scented soap to your very own rubber ducky! A super pet-friendly hotel, the Monaco not only provides a turn-down bone and nature videos for guests' furry roommates; they even have a dog concierge in their lobbies. Their complimentary late afternoon wine party in the lobby might include a handwriting psychic quietly reading palms for a small fee.

Customers love service that awakens their senses. Famous bars have become light shows, bakeries pump tantalizing aromas from their kitchens onto the sidewalk, and modern hospitals provide babbling fountains and tranquil music. Walk into the lobby of any Westin Hotel and your nose knows the scent suddenly shifts from the "smell of the street" to a signature fragrance called "White

"Do what you do so well that they will want to see it again and bring their friends."

-Walt Disney

Tea." An antique and memorabilia shop in Memphis plays oldies music; an upscale jewelry shop in Chicago has all employees wear formal evening attire.

And the 23 MPH perspective? It started out as a version of trivial pursuit—only it was related to minute facts everyone had collectively experienced at the end of a long weekend getaway. The setting was a gated beach resort; the participants were three couples who had rendezvoused from different locations. The stump-the-other-team trivia question that got the biggest laugh was, "What is the speed limit on the streets of this resort?" Everyone yelled, "23 MPH!" What made this speed limit sign so effective? A typical number would have just disappeared into the surroundings without being noticed. Stimulating the visual senses created a memory-making experience.

If you pull into Harry's Marathon Service station in Saline, Wisconsin, you can pump your own gas or have it pumped for you. But Charlie will take your money or your credit card and return your change and receipt. What makes this cashier unusual, however, is that Charlie is a golden retriever! Patrons to Harry's love Charlie's service so much that they started a 401K-9 retirement program for him. A book was even written about him called "Gas Station Charlie." (Note: Charlie died in 1999, but his son, Benjamin, follows in his father's paw prints).

A major hospital asked its patients during admission to identify their favorite flower. The hospital worked out an arrangement with a local florist to have a single stem of the patient's favorite flower in a bud vase placed on that returning patient's hospital bedside table.

Customers today are bored with ho-hum, pretty good, nothing-really-special service. They want their service experience to have a cherry on top! As customers, we like stimulation; we ignore bland. Finding innovative ways to make your service experience different from what others offer can be a key to building loyalty! When realtors suggest baking an apple pie before holding an open house and when upscale retail stores put a pianist at a baby grand on the sales floor, they are putting their "sense into service."

"They may forget what you said, but they will never forget how you made them feel."

-Carl W. Buechner

What can you do to follow the SPEED LIMIT 23 MPH Principle? Conduct a sense audit—what should your service experience smell like—sound like—feel like—look like—taste like if you wanted to excite your customers' memory with an enchanting experience? What messages are being sent by the color, font, tone, images, or language used on your website? What does your parking lot, lobby or waiting area telegraph about your attentiveness to your customers' experience? Examine your customers' experience through the lens of organizations known for a sensory-driven experience—Disney, Ringling Bros., or Cirque du Soleil. Service is memory-making; make yours out of the ordinary.

"Giving people a little more than they expect is a good way to get back a lot more than you would expect."

-Robert Half

Before and Beyond Service

The Circus Principle

$\mathcal{W}$hen the circus ringmaster wails, "...and children of all ages," he is speaking to me. I love the circus! When it came to my rural hometown when I was a boy, it was an all-consuming experience that embedded "circus" in my heart before it appeared and well beyond its departure.

Long before the circus train arrived, Ringling Bros. sent front men to my town to put stirring signs on telephone poles, place exciting ads in the local newspaper, and provide captivating materials for teachers to use in imparting lessons on circus animals. We watched men with large muscles and hammers put up the giant tent. The wild animals were paraded in colorful cages down Main Street. By the time the ticket booth opened, schools closed and businesses shut down so all could go to the circus! The whole town sat amazed at the funny clowns, thrilling trapeze and clever acts cavalcading under the big top. Outside there were fearless men, without shirts, swallowing knives and daredevil motorcycles racing around a small cage.

But, the experience did not end with the departure of the pretty lady riding on top of the jeweled elephant. We all took home a colorful souvenir providing us a perpetual memory of that special experience. We wore a grin for days and "circus" dominated our conversations in the school hallways and got reenacted on the playground! The "Circus Principle" is about a great customer experience created through the careful management of timing— before the main event and beyond the main event.

Customer experience is enhanced through anticipation—set with meticulous attention to optimizing buildup much like "enchanting service is coming to town." For example, the brass railing at Disney theme parks is polished in the middle of the night so guests never see it being cleaned. The Las Brisas Hotel in Acapulco cuts the grass after hours with manual clippers and engine-free push mowers so guests never hear the unpleasant sounds of maintenance underway.

Customer experience more likely remains embedded in memory if the experience extends beyond the engagement itself. Johnny Adair of A Brand New Look is my world-class hairstylist. The first time he cut my hair, he commented that not only was he interested in how it looked when I exited the barber chair, but he was also eager to ensure it looked great when I attempted to replicate his artistry in my bathroom the following day. So I got a short take-away lesson—much like a circus souvenir. Giving me a

hand mirror and turning the barber chair so the large wall mirror was behind me, he said, "I want you to watch how I style your hair so you'll know how to keep it looking exactly like it does when you leave here today."

Nordstrom is famous for stretching the service experience beyond the main event. "We try to guess what is beyond the customer's purchase," says John McClesky of the men's suits department at their Dallas store. "If a customer buys a sports jacket, the obvious extension might be a tie. But if you learn the customer is buying the jacket for a cruise, you might explore dressy shorts or an ascot." John continues, "But slipping a complimentary set of collar stays in the newly purchased jacket pocket (a frequently forgotten item on a trip) can leave a customer awed."

What can you do to follow the **CIRCUS** Principle? Anticipate what might ready your customer for his or her service encounter. Carefully think through potential wait time. Universal Orlando shows movies to entertain guests as they stand in the queue waiting for an attraction. On the opposite side of the encounter, lay out in your mind the possibilities of what customers will be doing, thinking and feeling after you have met their presented need. Instead of asking, "Will there be anything else?" ask "What have we not thought of that would make your hotel stay really special?" Make your queries reach into the future and the customer will provide you clues ripe for an occasional marvel.

"Be everywhere, do everything, and never fail
to astonish the customer."

-Macy's Motto

"Service is not a list of off-the-shelf solutions. It's a constant process of discovery. To be of real service, one must be willing to constantly discover exactly what the customer wants or needs—and then provide it."

-Mark Ursino, former Microsoft director

"The easiest and most powerful way to increase customer loyalty is really very simple. Make your customers happy. Just keep 'em smiling. Do that every day and your business will be fine."

-Kevin Stirtz

HARDWIRE WISDOM INTO SERVICE

The Campfire Story Principle

*J*unior Spivey always reminds me of a great campfire story—the ones with as much lesson as laughter. After we bought a getaway home on the banks of the Chattahoochee River in North Georgia, we needed someone to look after the place. Junior came very highly recommended.

Junior is from rural North Carolina, just over the state line. He would say he lives "in a holler by a crick close to my kin." He is as passionate and animated as the really good part of a campfire story. His accent—laced with charming expressions like "worsh," "thar," and "battree"—animate his language, making it sound more like a story than a conversation. Now before you go and read this as pejorative, you should know that I grew up in South Georgia; we Southerners take great pride in our dialect peculiarities.

The best part about Junior is his graduate education from the school of hard knocks. "Youins don't have 'nuff lime in your yard," he advised us. He had the demeanor of a physician who had just reviewed a patient's tests. We had asked a landscaper who thought adding lime was foolish. But Dr. Junior was not deterred. He took a few soil samples and sent them off to the state agricultural extension service. He brought us the predicted results—complete with complicated graphs—which he expertly explained. We never doubted Junior's know-how after that.

When deer selected our yard as the in-place for a late night snack, Junior swung into action. "Those dogwoods are pert-near gone," he told us one morning after a snack attack. Not only did he replace shrubs the deer raved about with new ones they avoided, but we were tutored on easy steps for making our yard a less fashionable watering hole for animals that enjoyed excavating our lawn for food—armadillos, possums, skunks and even wild pigs.

Customers love service providers that help them learn. While their confidence is amplified by smart, their receptivity is lowered by smart-aleck. Wisdom by a customer mentor is best conveyed in the spirit of a campfire story—nonjudgmentally, centered on the receiver, and warmed by compassion for the customer. It is sharing, much like a friend might offer a tip on where to catch the most fish. It is laced with as much attention to the learner-customer as to the expertise.

"Committed to helping men dress better than they have to." These words are the tag line of a radio ad for Pocket's Men's Wear in Dallas. Pocket's was founded over thirty years ago by David Smith, a longtime veteran of men's wear. Appalled by the bland way business professionals dressed for work, he opened his own store to unfold a dream of making men's fashion matter— and matter deeply—to lawyers, bankers and other professionals. His goal was for his salespeople to be fashion consultants and clothing mentors to their customers. These same people give seminars to professional associations' members on how to dress for achievement.

The fact that they have several tailors standing by gives customers the assurance that their unique requirements will be met in a hurry.

What can you do to use the CAMPFIRE STORY Principle? Be a customer mentor. Be more of an escort to insight and discovery than an expert with information. Look for artifacts in the customer's experience that can be turned into devices for learning—a Styrofoam coffee cup with a teaching point printed on it or an FAQ (frequently asked questions) sheet to accompany a product the customer purchases. If a world-class mentor ran your business for a week, how would it improve? Change call center farewells from a closed-ended "Is there anything else I can help you with?" to an open-ended "What else can I help you learn more about today?"

Customers love to learn if the journey is more like a story than like a chore.

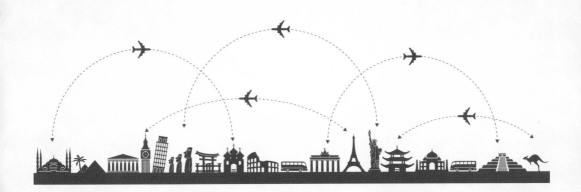

MONOGRAM THE MOMENT

The Fly-Fishing Principle

*I*t looked like we were going to have to spend the night in the car with the cat! Not a good idea! We were traveling to South Texas and had targeted Austin as our halfway overnight destination. We realized two hours out that we had no hotel reservation on a Friday night UT football weekend. Plus, we travel with our cat. We called the usual hotels—Marriott, Hilton, Holiday Inn, Motel Six—all with the same response, "Sorry, no pets!"

"Why don't we call the Four Seasons Hotel?" my wife suggested. I thought, "Oh, no. Three hundred dollars a night!" When she sensed my resistance, she coyly asked, "What if we just called them to see what they say?"

You know where this story is going! "We'd love to have your cat," the front desk clerk sang into the phone. "What's your kitty's name? We want to register your little kitty."

"Taco," my wife answered, "Taco Bell!"

When we arrived at the Four Seasons there was practically a welcoming party—all eager to greet THE cat. After the "oo's and ah's" we arrived at our gorgeous lakefront guest room. The hotel staff had already set out a serving tray with a logoed bowl for cat food, another for water, and a small cat toy. My wife was super happy, Taco was super happy, but I was still not liking this pricey event.

But the monogrammed moment came the next morning when we ordered room service breakfast. When the bellman knocked on our door, Taco immediately jumped to the middle of the bed. As the bellman entered the room with our breakfast, what do you think were the first words out of his mouth? You guessed it! "Good morning, Taco!"

As soon as the room door closed, I could hear my credit card cry. My wife swooned, "I'll never stay anywhere but a Four Seasons hotel. If the room service guy knows the name of my cat, why would I stay anywhere else?"

Customers love monogrammed service. Monogrammed service is a lot like fly-fishing for trout. Most fish are complete suckers for a juicy worm on a hook dangling in front of their face below a cork floating above on the surface of the water. Not trout. Trout, like customers, prefer a monogrammed adventure. You must carefully study what the trout are eating, buy or fashion a fly to mimic their cuisine, authentically present the fly to the trout, and the moment you get a bite, slowly draw the trout to a net because what separates you from the trout is a line slightly larger than a thread.

Please don't push this metaphor too far. There are parts of a fishing metaphor that do not work when it comes to great customer service—like hook, catch, or reeling in. But regular fishing is to fly-fishing what whittling might be to scrimshaw or what baking pre-sliced cookies might be to gourmet confectionary baking! Fly-fishing is all about personalization—with a fish instead of a person!

Monogramming service requires time and care; it cannot be a knee-jerk or fast-track response. It is unique to the customer and it must always be sincere and authentic. Customers know if your brand of service is a trick, an empty gesture, or a selfish ploy. When service is genuinely personalized, it reminds customers they are vitally present in an important service relationship. Having customers' names on an offering or their needs embedded in it, informs customers they are valued recipients, not just typical end-users.

Order personalized award ribbons from the Award Company of America in Tuscaloosa, Alabama, and your order comes with a thank-you note that contains the words, "I am the machine operator who actually made your ribbons. I am very proud of my work. We want to give you highly personal service. If you are dissatisfied for any reason, please contact our customer service department. They will contact me and I will personally correct any problem. Thank you for your order. We look forward to receiving your next order."

"We wildly underestimate the power of the tiniest personal touch."

-Tom Peters

Celebration West, a Dallas restaurant famous for its lively ambiance and surprising frivolity, has waiters applaud when a repeat customer enters the restaurant. That might be an embarrassing gesture at a four-star fancy place, but it fits well with their wildness.

Manheim, a large wholesale auto auction company, gets rave reviews from their non-native U.S. customers by flying a United Nations-like row of national flags at their auctions frequented by auto exporters—one for each country represented by the customers who frequent that auction.

What can you do to apply the FLY-FISHING Principle? Display the upbeat attitude you want your customers to have. Never let customers leave disappointed. As they do at Starbucks, repeat customers' names often so you will know them when they return. Even if you can't always give customers what they want, you can always give them a great service experience. Use the optimistic attitude of, "The answer is 'yes' what's the question?" Listen to learn, not to make a point. Customers will indirectly tell you ways to personalize their experience.Thank customers like you really mean it. And never forget they have options. Customers feel valued when you show you never forget that fact either.

"Nobody cares how much you know
until they know how much you care."

-Theodore Roosevelt

"Biggest question: Isn't it really 'customer helping' rather than customer service? And wouldn't you deliver better service if you thought of it that way?"

-Jeffrey Gitomer

"No one ever attains very eminent success by simply doing what is required; it is the amount and excellence of what is over and above the required that determines the greatness of ultimate distinction."

-Charles Francis Adams

"Our greatest asset is the customer! Treat each customer as if they are the only one!"

-Laurice Leitao

"One customer, well taken care of, could be more valuable than $10,000 worth of advertising."

-Jim Rohn

Effort Removal Squared

The Easy Button Principle

*L*ate one Sunday evening at my desk, I was online ordering promotional visors from Stitch America in Bremen, Georgia. I had selected the visor color, style, and words to be stitched in a particular font and thread color. After loading in my credit card information, I sent the order off into cyberspace. I was about to turn out the light to go to bed when I received a text message on my smart phone, "Mr. Bell, are you still up? May I call you about the order you just placed?" I responded, "Yes." Within less than a minute, the phone rang. "This is Tonya. Thanks so much for your order. I want to give you superfast turnaround, but I want to make sure you get exactly what you wanted." I was thrilled! Someone cared on a late Sunday night about an online order. "The font size you have chosen will be too hard to read. May I suggest doubling it? I can send you a PDF photo showing the front of the visor in the actual size." I agreed, hung up the phone, and went to bed.

When I turned on my computer early the next morning, there was the PDF from Tonya. With it came a short e-mail note, "As soon as you give me the word that this is the best-looking visor you have ever seen, I will get it into production." Two days later I got an e-mail and text message from the production department that the visors were finished and being packaged for shipment. Later that day, I got an e-mail with a photocopy of the tracking order. Two days later a follow-up e-mail came indicating that their system showed the order had been delivered. Then Tonya called again. "Are you totally thrilled with your order?" I totally was! And the Stitch America service made me want to give up shopping centers forever.

Effort has become the big kahuna in customer experience. As customers, we abhor hassle, wait and aggravation that seem to add no value. We want convenience and freedom from stress more than almost any feature of service. We text instead of e-mail, pick the ATM over the branch lobby and make fast food our main culinary staple. We despise getting transferred or having to punch lots of numbers on the phone to get what we need. And short 9-5 office hours leave us eager to find a service provider with around-the-clock service.

My friend, Sue Cook, was late for her flight and had to quickly check out of the Ritz-Carlton Buckhead in Atlanta. The desk clerk went to another counter, completed the transaction and returned. Only then did Sue realize she was standing at the concierge desk rather than the front desk. When she apologized for the early morning mistake, the desk clerk warmly said, "Don't be silly, Ms. Cook, you can check out anywhere you like."

I needed the "Easy Button Principle" once when I was in desperate need of a plumber. New to the area, I just randomly picked one out of the Yellow Pages. Minutes later, the candidate for resolving my plumbing glitches arrived. "You called for a plumber," he said with obvious pride, "And I'm your man!" I was beginning to realize my plumbing gremlins were in very deep trouble. Five minutes later, he was outlining the problem, the prognosis, and the price. He obviously knew his stuff.

"I can fix it now—it's going to take me an hour and a half—or I can come back when it's more convenient. I'll take care of everything. When I'm done you'll have no cleanup and I guarantee my work for the rest of your life. You can pay me when I'm finished or I can e-mail or mail you an invoice."

Exactly 80 minutes later, I was writing a check and requesting business cards to give to my friends should they have plumbing trials. I had played "Yellow Pages roulette" in search of a plumber and hit the jackpot!

What can you do to show customers the EASY BUTTON? Create options for self-service but always with quick, easy access to a live person. Look at all service processes through your customers' eyes. Examine all service encounters with your anxiety meter and find ways to remove the angst from each customer's experience. If you can't reduce customer wait, manage the perception of wait as a bank does when it puts a TV in the teller line for customers to watch as they wait. Treat your colleagues like your most important customer.

"It is always the simple that produces the marvelous."

-Amelia Barr

Turn an "Oops" Into an Opportunity

The Panning for Gold Principle

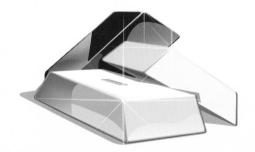

"*Y*ou people lied to me!!" Her biting words bounced off the walls of the customer waiting room. Customers were startled out of their seats. I was one! I thought of that old line: "Hell hath no fury like a...."

"I am so glad you came to me," the service person said with noticeable confidence. He moved closer to her and aimed his best eye contact straight at her livid face. "Would you be willing to tell me the details?" he said, world-class concern oozing from his voice.

"Mister, I'll tell everybody up your chain of command if I have to." Her mean junkyard dog style had bit down on a sympathetic ear and she was not about to let go.

"I don't want to miss any of this," the service person said, unshaken by her rage. "Could we please move in here so I can give you my complete attention?" He ushered her into an office away from the waiting area—and probably away from the object of her irritation.

None of us heard the conversation at the other end of the hallway. Oh, we all talked about his shoes, her loose screw, and his grace under pressure. Ten minutes later they emerged from down the hall. "Why can't they all be like you?" were her parting words as the waiting room door closed behind her.

I was lucky. I later got the same service person, giving me the opportunity to learn of his winning magic. "It's no big deal," he shrugged. "We all have our bad days. Today was hers. Since she's one of our customers, she deserves my best effort at fixing her problem—and her pain." His too-good-to-be-true flair seemed way too distinctive for me to let it go.

"So you think the customer is always right?" I pressed.

"Oh no," he said, resigning himself to the fact that he was going to be interviewed! "The customer is the customer—a regular person, just like me, right and wrong. I try to deal with a difficult customer just like I try to do when my son or wife or neighbor is being difficult." He handed me my receipt with one last piece of wisdom: "It is not about who's right, it's about making the customer feel right."

Customers don't expect you to be perfect; they do expect you to care when things go wrong. How you demonstrate that care is a lot like panning for gold.

"Problems are good, not bad. Welcome them and become the solution."

- Mark Victor Hansen

Panning for gold starts with a double handful of sand in a steel pan dipped in the water and filled half full. Next, the pan is moved back and forth so small amounts of yellow sand can wash over the side.

But this is the point where panning for gold gets real serious. Impatience or strong arming the way the pan is shaken means the black sand (with the gold) escapes over the side along with the yellow sand. Once black sand is the only sand left in the pan, you are rewarded with flecks of gold that reside among its grains.

Turning customer disdain into delight is like panning for gold among the sand. And like sand, service can come in a black form—those dark, disappointing moments that cause customers to doubt your caring. How you handle "the dark sand" can be the difference between losing a customer over the side and turning a customer "oops" into the opportunity for gold (aka loyalty).

Michael Graze had been looking forward to his birthday party. He and his mom had planned it in great detail, inviting his school pals. So when the six-year-old's Power Rangers birthday cake from the local H-E-B grocery store arrived with Michael spelled "M-I-C-H-E-L-E" he was distraught. The great centerpiece of the party had turned into an object of derision through a spelling error! He swore he could never show his face in school again.

When H-E-B staff member Julie McCoy heard of Michael's distress from his mother, she didn't hesitate. First, she was completely honest and took full accountability for the error. Knowing that apologies and refunds would be small solace for a little boy's crushed spirit, she arranged for a new cake and a new party—this one at a local children's amusement park, with Michael as host and H-E-B footing the bill.

What can you do to apply the PANNING FOR GOLD Principle? Great service recovery takes humility and compassion that lets an angry customer know you are there to fix, not fight. It requires focusing on the gold in the customers—not their anger on the surface. Anger is an expression of fear. Much like comforting a child after a bad dream, managing a customer's perceived betrayal means taking time to understand, empathize and mine the customer's expectations so a good solution is found. "Gold finding" recovery means helping customers feel even more faithful after a hiccup.

"Our greatest glory is not in never failing, but in rising up every time we fail."

- Ralph Waldo Emerson

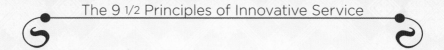
"A lot of people have fancy things to say about customer service, but it's just a day-in, day-out, ongoing, never-ending, unremitting, persevering, compassionate kind of activity."

- Leon A. Gorman

"The creative act, the defeat of habit by originality, overcomes everything."

- George Lois

"Breakthroughs come from an instinctive judgment of what customers might want if they knew to think about it."

- Andrew Grove, CEO, Intel

Synergize Your Service Delivery

The Fruit Salad Principle

*Y*ou walk through the entrance and a big fuzzy-costumed character greets you. Everywhere you look there are smiling employees and happy guests. As you wind through the colorfully adorned passageway, a mechanical rooster pops up and sings to the mechanical hens in the nearby cage. A peppy soundtrack is periodically punctuated by an announcement that the show in one section is about to begin. The smell of fresh popcorn hits you as in a county fair. Think you are in a theme park? Nope! You are in a grocery store—one of four Stew Leonard's farm fresh food stores in Connecticut and New York—which has been called the Disneyland of Dairy Stores by *The New York Times*!

Stew has masterfully created a setting for surprise. Kids are treated like future customers, from the petting zoo outside to receiving a free ice cream cone if their parents spend $100. Frequent customers get warm hugs as if they had just showed up at a family reunion. If something leaves a customer disappointed, employees are taught to practice customer service rule #1 carved on a giant 6,000 pound rock at the store entrance: "The customer is always right." And the payoff? Stew Leonard's is the most successful grocery store in the world, listed in the *Guinness Book of World Records* as having the highest retail sales per square foot of any grocery establishment in the world. The company was rated in *Fortune* magazine's "100 Best Companies to Work For" for ten consecutive years.

Stew Leonard is a great example of the Fruit Salad principle—a scrumptious mix of several of the nine principles. You can go online and listen to the Farm Fresh Five after hearing them perform at the store. Stew hosts free Haybale Theater family movie nights during the month of October. The Cow Cam teaches you unique facts; the easy recipes (in the store and on their website) provide clever cooking lessons from "My Daughter Blake's Chicken" to "Halloween Pumpkin-Sage Soup."

And, it is not just reserved for brick and mortar establishments. Online businesses can adopt the Fruit Salad principle as well.

The daughter of one of my business partners ordered a CD for her child from CD Baby. Below is the e-mail her daughter received after the order was shipped:

Your CD has been gently taken from our CD Baby shelves with sterilized contamination-free gloves and placed onto a satin pillow. A team of 50 employees inspected your CD and polished it to make sure it was in the best possible condition before mailing. Our world-renowned packing specialist lit a local artisan candle and a hush fell over the crowd as he put your CD into the finest gold-lined box that money can buy.

We all had a wonderful celebration afterwards and the whole party marched down the street to the post office where the entire town of Portland waved "Bon Voyage!" to your package, on its way to you, in our private CD Baby jet on this day, March 25, 2011.

We hope you had a wonderful time shopping at CD Baby. In commemoration, we have placed your picture on our wall as "Customer of the Year." We're all exhausted but can't wait for you to come back to CDBABY.COM!! Thank you, thank you, thank you! Sigh...We miss you already. We'll be right here at http://cdbaby.com/, patiently awaiting your return.

How can you apply the FRUIT SALAD Principle? Get a group of colleagues together. Ask each to take one of the nine principles and meet prepared to identify two ways to apply their assigned principle. Together, pick the four best ideas and then brainstorm ways to combine them! Pick your favorite service exemplar—one known for delighted customers. Imagine what might change if that person was in charge of your customer experience for a week. Looking through new eyes can arm you with new perspectives leading to innovative practices.

We end our ride with a powerful concept—the more principles you can appropriately build into your customer's experience, the more likely it will be experienced as exceptional rather than expected, remarkable rather than routine. It means decorating the experience as you are delivering it. It takes service with passion—passing your best from you to your customers! When you give your customers the best that you have, their best will come back to you!

"The goal as a company is to have customer service that is not just the best, but legendary."

–Sam Walton

"There are no traffic jams along the extra mile."

-Roger Staubach

About the Author

Chip R. Bell

Chip R. Bell is a senior partner with the Chip Bell Group and manages their office near Atlanta. He has served as consultant, trainer, or speaker to such major organizations as GE, Microsoft, Marriott, Lockheed-Martin, Cadillac, KeyBank,

Ritz-Carlton Hotels, Eli Lilly, USAA, Merrill Lynch, Cornell University, Allstate, Caterpillar, Hertz, Accenture, Verizon Wireless, Harley-Davidson and Victoria's Secret. Additionally, he was a highly decorated infantry unit commander in Vietnam with the elite 82nd Airborne.

Chip is the author or coauthor of nineteen books, many of them national best-sellers. Some of his previous books include *Wired and Dangerous* (co-authored with John Patterson and a winner of a 2011 Axiom Award as well as a 2012 Independent Publishers IPPY Award), *Take Their Breath Away* (also with John Patterson), *Managers as Mentors* (with Marshall Goldsmith), *Magnetic Service* (with Bilijack Bell and winner of the 2004 Benjamin Franklin Award), *Managing Knock Your Socks Off Service* (with Ron Zemke), *Service Magic* (also with Ron Zemke) and *Customers as Partners*. He has appeared live on CNBC, CNN, Fox Business Network and ABC and his work has been featured in *Fortune, Business Week, Forbes, The Wall Street Journal, USA Today, Inc. Magazine* and *Fast Company*.

For more information about Chip visit www.chipbell.com

7 GREAT WAYS to Use Our Gift Books

PERSONAL APPLICATIONS

1. Personal inspiration

2. A gift that keeps on giving

3. Birthday gift for friends, family or co-workers

4. A thank you gift

5. Provide encouragement for a friend or family member

6. A Mother's Day or Father's Day gift

7. A Graduation gift

BUSINESS APPLICATIONS

1. Reinforce your meeting theme with a motivational "take away"

2. Thank your best customers

3. Reinforce your corporate culture

4. A memorable gift

5. Motivate your sales team

6. Send to your best prospects

7. Invest in your team's personal development